BEHIND THE V

Portraits of a Norfolk Village
Bressingham, Then and Now

Photographs by
Elizabeth Handy

Typeset by DP Photosetting, Aylesbury, Bucks
Origination, Printing and Binding in Singapore
under the supervision of MRM Graphics Ltd., Winslow, Bucks.

CONTENTS

	Page
Introduction	**4**
The People in My View, *then and now.*	**9**
The Buildings and their People, *then and now.*	**17**
The Houses and their People, *then and now.*	**41**
The Groups and their People, *then and now.*	**57**
The Work and the People, *then and now.*	**73**

The Work that is no longer

The Work that stays the same

The Work that is new

| **Conclusion** | **103** |
| **Acknowledgements** | **106** |

INTRODUCTION

This is me, **Elizabeth Handy**
the eye behind the camera.

Born at the beginning of the War, an Army daughter, I lived in many homes
in many countries in my youth. I came to Bressingham over twenty years ago
and felt properly at home at last, dividing my life now between there and
London. I have been a professional portrait photographer for the last ten
years, having earlier been an interior designer, a counsellor and, always,
mother to Kate and Scott, wife and partner to Charles.

My hope is that my portraits show people as they like themselves to be, and
that this small book can be a reminder that each of us is different, but also
special in our own way, and that it is the mix of our differences which keep
any view, or any village, alive.

I live in Bressingham, a village near Diss in South Norfolk. The view I look at cannot have changed in 100 years. The village, too, still has most of the buildings and the institutions which it had 100 years ago. The 13th. Century Church is still there, as is the School, the Pub, the Shop, the Mill, the Hall, the Rectory, the Grange, along with most of the old farmhouses and cottages. The village clubs and committees are still there, as they have always been. 765 people lived there in 1911 and 690 lived there at the latest census. The view, in other words, is much the same to-day as it was when the century began.

Behind the view, however, the way things work has changed a lot. They farm the fields in front of me quite differently today. The people who live in the old houses, farms and cottages are different too. Most of the old names have gone, replaced by new names who lead different lives and do different work, in ways unimaginable 100 years ago, although they still live in the same old houses and use the same village buildings.

Remarkably, the village seems to have gone straight from the agricultural age to the information age without the intervening industrial age, thus allowing the outward things to remain the same while much has changed behind. Like a well-darned sock, it still looks the same, still works as well, although much of the old wool has been replaced by newer stuff. In a way, the story of my village carries a message for society - to keep things the same, much has got to change.

This book is my personal portrait of the changes, and also of the things that have not changed. It is my own record of some of the people who have, in their varied ways, kept my view alive. It is not meant as any sort of history, or as a survey of the village, but as my own tribute to an enduring place which has been an important part of my life.

THE PEOPLE IN MY VIEW
then, and now

When I came to live at Old Hall Cottages, in 1972, the land around belonged to Three Gates Farm, and was farmed, in the traditional way, largely by hand, by Charlie and Jim Fellingham and their sister, Hilda. As far as I could tell, nothing much had changed in the view in front of me since the beginning of the century, nor had the way of farming changed all that much. Charlie's tractor, bought in 1956 and still going, just, in 1995, had replaced the horse-drawn plough, but the straw was still stacked by hand, the beet cut with a sickle, the grass scythed by Jim and the butter churned by Hilda's patient hands.

Jim died in 1991, Charlie in 1995, at the age of 89, and Hilda retired from making her butter and cream, and from rearing her hens and chickens, some years before that. Hilda still lives in the old farmhouse, but the land is now farmed for her by Paul and John Brooke with all the latest in modern machinery. The field in my view still grows the same crops, but whereas at the beginning of the century two men cut the corn with a scythe, at the rate of one acre a day, Paul now harvests the whole field in half a day and John, unaided, transfers the straw to the stack.

The increase in productivity and the move to contracting are symptomatic of what is happening everywhere, not just in farming. The end product may look the same, but the way it is produced has changed radically, and that has changed our lives.

The view from my window in 1972, when I first saw it . . .
and still the same in 1996.

Charlie.

Jim.

Hilda, churning butter.

Now – John.

Now – Paul.

CHANGING TIMES

Electricity comes to Bressingham

Electricity first came to Bressingham in the 1950's.
Viola Walker tells the story of her grandfather's cousin, Herbert Pearce, retired farmer, who lived in a bungalow near Pillar Box Corner with Alice his wife. The Pearces were excited by the prospect of electricity and the difference it would make to their lives, and on the day when it was finally connected they waited in anticipation for the dawning of the light.

Nothing happened! The next day they asked the electrician what had gone wrong. He explained to them, then, that if they wanted the light to come on they had first to put a bulb in the light fitting!

THE BUILDINGS, AND THEIR PEOPLE
then, and now

The principal buildings of the village, the Church, the Pub, the Village Shop, the School and the Mill, which grinds the grain from the farms - these still exist, and still serve the same purposes that they did a century ago. The people who work in them, however, reflect our changing times. The village Rector now has four parishes to look after, the pub is part of a chain and the mill is owned by an American corporation. The school is thriving, but, to-day, caters for a much wider catchment area, something made possible by better transport.

The greater prosperity of life to-day shows up in the photos of the schoolchildren, while the occupations of the Parish Council and the Churchwardens mark the move away from an agricultural society, one in which women's work happened mostly in the home. Institutions can be immortal, unlike those who live and work in them, but only if they change with the times.

THE CHURCH – c. 1930 *and Now*

The Church, first built in 1280 and again in 1526, is as it as always been, minus a few elm trees and plus some tombstones.

THE RECTOR – in 1940

Canon Nock was Rector of Bressingham for over fifty-two years until his death in 1960. Here he is photographed at his wedding.

THE RECTOR – *Now*

David Hunter is Rector, today, of Bressingham and three other parishes. He lives in the new modern Rectory. His family comes from Kent.

THE CHURCHWARDENS – *Then*

The Parish records show that, until recently, the Churchwardens were always farmers or the wives of farmers.

Paul and Barbara Brooke were both Churchwardens, at one time or another, for many years. Paul has farmed in Bressingham for over forty-five years and now works with his son John.

THE CHURCHWARDENS – *Now*

Ted Mercer – previously the agricultural research co-ordinator for a pharmaceutical company, then the regional representative of an insurance firm and, in his spare time, devoted to his pigs. He is seen here with Sue, his wife.

Hilary Hammond – Director of Arts and Sciences for the County and, in his spare time, a serious cook.

THE PAROCHIAL CHURCH COUNCIL – *Now*

Only one is a farmer. Almost half are women.

The Stores, Bressingham.

THE VILLAGE SHOP – c. 1930
and Now

The posts, for hitching the horses, have gone. The bricks have been plastered and painted and the trees have grown. It was, then, one of three shops and a post office. Now, the other shops have gone and the post office has moved here. It continues to be, as it has always been, the centre of the village communications network.

Peter Harries runs it to-day, with his wife Pam.

THE PUB – c. l930 *and Now*

The Green which used to link the Church and Pub has given way to a busy main road. The pub has changed its name and its owners, who have restored its traditional interior.

Paul Simpson (centre) is Commercial Director of the Company which owns this and other country pubs. **Ken and Frankie Horn** are the current licensees.

THE MILL – *Then and Now*

The Mill still stands where it always did, but the wind sails went in 1930 and the place has expanded ever since. The Burroughes family has been replaced as the owners, after three generations, by an American Corporation.

Eric Burroughes, the last owner-manager

Stephen Howlett, the current manager.

The School, Bressingham.

THE SCHOOL – c. 1930 *and Now*

The curriculum may have changed and the classes grown but boys and girls still start their formal schooling here as they have always done.

Alan Huckle, the Headmaster today.

The Girls – c. 1913.

The Girls – *Now*

c. 1928

38

Now

39

CHANGING TIMES

"Courting"

Jeff Harvey, who has lived in Bressingham since 1962, told me of his friend John Pollard's analysis of the changing radius of courting. In his grandfather's day, the only way to get about for the average villager was by walking along the footpaths which connected the farms and the shops. Courting was confined to the village or, at most, the next-door one. Then came the bicycle, solid tyres and all, which allowed his father to venture farther afield. By John's time the motor car increased the possibilities enormously and, to-day, the aeroplane and even the Internet make it possible to 'court' a partner the other side of the world.

THE HOUSES, AND THEIR PEOPLE
then, and now

The old houses and farmhouses of the village still look much as they always did, although the tell-tale signs of modern life intrude here and there. The people who live in them, however, are evidence of the way life and work in the village has changed.

The Rector no longer lives in what was the Rectory but is now re-named The Lodge, the Grange is home to an executive in an automobile firm, the Hall is the centre of a large plant business, what was a farmhouse is now the doctor's family home, and my own cottage, once the home for two families, is now the home and workplace of a writer and a photographer. Where once every farmhouse was the centre of a farm, now the few that still are true farmhouses stand out as the exceptions.

New people have brought continued life to the old houses, but, despite all the changes that have happened inside, the view outside remains the same. This blend of change and continuity in the older houses of the village has helped, maybe, to make the changes that come with modern life less obtrusive and less alarming.

The Highlands, Bressingham.

THE HIGHLANDS – c. 1930
and Now

Electricity and a Bottle Bank intrude on the Highlands to-day. Once a farm, it is now the home of **Angela Child** and her husband, Christopher who, from here, works as a travel consultant and tour manager. They moved here from Kent three years ago.

The Grange, Bressingham.

THE GRANGE – c. 1930 *and Now*

Once a farm, now the home of **Kenneth Sears**, an automotive design engineer at Lotus, and **Lyn**, his wife. They moved here three years ago.

THE HALL – c. 1890 *and Now*

Sold as a 200 acre 'shooting estate' in 1946, the Hall is now the centre of Bressingham Gardens, a plant nursery, showpiece garden and steam railway museum.

It is the home, today, of **Alan Bloom** who started it all 50 years ago.

FOLLY FARM – c. 1910 *and Now*

Unchanged on the outside, the house was, as its name suggests, the centre of a working farm. It is, now, the home of **Nigel Thompson**, the local doctor, **Penny**, his wife, and their family, **Coralie**, **Ben**, **Amelia**, **Sophie**, with Jamie, the pony.

THE RECTORY – c. 1910 *and Now*

Then it was The Rectory and the home of the Rector. Now it is Bressingham Lodge and the home of **Marianne and John Dane**, both retired now, but previously a teacher and the Finance Director of a local electrical engineering company.

OLD BOYLAND HALL – c. 1919
and Now

Once a farm and still, unusually for the village, a farm, and the home of **Rosemary and Maurice Brown**, whose son, John, and grandson, David, now work the farm as well as the adjoining property.

OLD HALL COTTAGES – c. 1910 *and Now*

Formerly the front door of the cottage home of the Noble family, whose son, Willie (on the left) lived there until we moved in and I turned their one living room into my study.

CHANGING TIMES

"Schooling"

Arthur Pearce went to Bressingham School in the early years of the century. Bright though he was, he had to leave at 13 and got his first job working as odd job man for the Headmaster of Diss Grammar School, who encouraged him to take up photography as a hobby. After the war Arthur returned to Bressingham and joined his father as a carpenter.

Arthur's daughter, Viola, also went to Bressingham School but then went on to Diss Grammar School after passing her 11 + . There were three career opportunities open to girls then – nursing, teaching or working for the Norwich Union. She chose the latter.

Viola's two sons went to University, one getting a degree in law and the other in chemistry. Neither Viola nor her sons live in Bressingham.

THE GROUPS, AND THEIR PEOPLE
then, and now

Village life has always hinged around its clubs, societies, groups and committees, some of them social, some sportive and some with a specific purpose, such as the organization of the annual Flower Show.

There were clubs and committees then, just as there are now, but with subtle changes in their functions and their membership. It seems that, in the past, the men were mostly too busy on the land to have much time for team sports, which were represented, then, by the women's stoolball team and, now, by the men's cricket team.

The Ladies' Club still thrives, but the ladies of to-day are not only very differently attired, they also, mostly, have jobs outside the home, which perhaps explains why there is no longer any call for a Sewing Group for the younger women. On the other hand there are now more elderly people, and a Silver Thread Club to cater for them. Ad hoc groups still arise when needed, the team who restored the church clock, then, and the team who raised the money and then restored, replaced and rehung the peal of bells in the church. The bells rang out on Christmas Eve 1995 for the first time in 100 years.

The ability to "organize around enthusiasms" is one of the bonding mechanisms of a good society. It provides people with a 'third place', over and above the family and the workplace. My village may have changed its enthusiasms over the years but has never lost the capacity to organize around them.

THE LADIES CLUB – c. 1910

Meeting at the Rectory.

THE LADIES CLUB – *Now*

Meeting at what is now Bressingham Lodge, in front of the same window.

None of the people in this photograph was born in the village, and most of them have or have had paid work outside the home.

Bressingham Musical Society. 1918.

1918 – THE MUSICAL SOCIETY

Now – **THE DRAMA GROUP**

c. 1920 – THE SEWING GROUP

Now – THE PLAYGROUP

STOOLBALL CLUB 1915 BRESSINGHAM

1915 – THE STOOLBALL TEAM

Now – **THE CRICKET TEAM**

1931 – THE CHURCH CLOCK TEAM
who installed the clock

Now – THE BELL RESTORATION COMMITTEE
who restored, replaced and rehung the original peal of bells and added two new bells.

And also

Now – **THE FLOWER SHOW COMMITTEE**

Now – **THE SILVER THREAD CLUB**

And, both Then and Now

THE PARISH COUNCIL

The first Parish Council met in the nineteenth century, and the minute book with the records of its meetings still exists.

In 1897 there were, on the Council, 4 Farmers, 1 Thatcher and 2 Labourers, all male.

In 1995 there were still 2 Farmers, but also now 4 Business Executives, 1 Teacher, 1 Plantsman and 1 lorry driver. 3 of these were women.

THE WORK, AND THE PEOPLE
then, and now

The village is set amid the cornfields of East Anglia. In the past, the work of almost everyone in the village was connected with the land in some way or another. Now, to work on the land, except in your own garden for pleasure, is rare. Only three farmers are featured in this book and they are almost all that there are. The children of the agricultural workers of the past have learnt new skills and have, most of them, left the village to find new work in the towns and cities. Few of the old family names still survive.

Others have, however, moved in from the towns and the cities to replace them, bringing with them work that is new to the village, some of it traditional, such as garden design or dog breeding, writing or editing, but some of it reflecting the new world of computers and the information age. Much of this work can be done from home or at home, like the mother of seven children who also runs an au pair agency covering the whole country from her one-time farmhouse home.

Those who worry that the fading of the agricultural age will mean the end of village life should note how the new forms of work are often well suited to a village base. Now that many jobs can be done anywhere, people will often bring the work to where they want to live instead of having to move to where the work is. If the village is a place where life is good, work can increasingly follow.

THE WORK THAT IS NO LONGER

c. 1914 – **George Hoskins, a soldier**
killed in the first World War, as were 12 others in the village.

THE. FORGE. BRESSINGHAM

c. 1910 – **The Knapper**

who filled in the holes in the roads for which the village was responsible, working outside the blacksmith's forge, long gone from the village, as have the two cobblers who used to work there.

Philip Maiden (centre) who worked as Groom to Canon Knock, pictured here between Herbert Butler who took many of the old photographs in this book and George Morley, a neighbouring smallholder.

THE WORK THAT STAYS THE SAME

Now – **Vera Francis, the Church organist**
as she has been for 43 years, also mother of six, grandmother of ten.

Now – **Stephen Hubbard** who still cares for what was once his father's smallholding but also runs his own building business.

c. 1920 – **Arthur Pearce, carpenter**
repairing a cartwheel, the agricultural machinery of its day.

Now – **John Hubbard, a mechanical engineer,**
running his own business servicing agricultural machinery and automobiles.

c. 1910 – **The Village postman.**

Now – **Christopher Ray, our postman,**
at the same Pillar Box Corner.

c. 1910 – **Nellie Noble, Mother of six,**
who lived in one part of my cottage.

Now – **Naomi Rawlings, Mother of seven**
who also runs an agency for au pairs and nannies from her home, with **Nick**, the father, who runs a design and advertising business in the local town, seen here with Byron, India, Ross, Bruce, Brooke, Jade, Paige and Jaffa, the cat.

***Now* – Rodger and Millie Aves**
are a comparative rarity, these days, a farming family, from three generations of farmers at The Oaks, farming with their son, Desmond (the group above shows Rodger's grandfather, in front of the same window, at the wedding of his daughter).

THE WORK THAT IS NEW

Now – **Charles Handy**, an author, who turned a labourer's cottage into a writer's retreat.

Now – **Pat Bateson**, who edits scientific textbooks and journals from her farmhouse home.

Now – **Deborah Kellaway**
turned a one acre field into a showpiece garden 30 years ago and is, today, a writer of books on gardening.

Now – **Gladys Knott**, a nurse, and now Bressingham Parish's first lay reader.

Now – **Cynthia Mann**
changed a group of pig sties into dog kennels 30 years ago to run her dog training
business. With Shadow.

Now – **Michael Reynolds**, international lawyer, commuting between Brussels and Bressingham, and **David Neville**, psychotherapist.

Now – **Angela Griffiths**, a Cosmetics Representative, married to a freelance electrical engineer, who travels the world, pictured here with **Guy and Emma**.

Now – **David Craggs**, self-employed systems analyst, currently contracted to British Telecom, with **Sue**, a nurse and **Alice and William**.

Now – **Harris Marks**, systems analyst for a Japanese Bank, commuting daily to London, with **Nicola**, consultant to Norfolk County Council.

Now – **Chris Beesley**, telecommunications design engineer with Hewlett Packard, and **Julie**, publishing editor at Jarrolds, with John, their son, pictured here in the Churchyard while Chris was working on the Bell Restoration Project.

CONCLUSION

While much has changed, much has stayed the same. The view from the church tower, (overleaf), with the field I look at in the distance, has changed little over the last 85 years.

The village, however, has now spread well beyond this view. New people have brought new skills and new life to old places.

I have only been able to photograph a small selection of the 690 people of the village, but there are enough portraits here, I hope, to demonstrate how change and continuity combine to keep a place, and a view, alive.

c. 1910

Now.

Acknowledgements

I would like to thank all the many people in Bressingham, as well as those from farther afield, who have been so generous with their time and help. I would like to thank, particularly, those people who have agreed to be photographed and who either appear in this book or, sadly, do not because of restricted space. Then there are those who have shared old photographs of their homes and families with me, as well as their stories and nuggets of information. I am grateful to them all for letting me into the lives of themselves and their families.

My special thanks go to my neighbour, **Charlie Butler**, who first showed me the photographs of Bressingham, taken by his father over eighty five years ago, photographs which first inspired me to take my portraits of the village to-day. Charlie's patient help and courtesy was invaluable. I must also pay my respects to two Bressingham photographers of the past, some of whose photographs appear in this book: **Herbert Butler**, the father of Charlie Butler, and **Arthur Pearce**, carpenter, member of the church choir for 70 years and enthusiastic photographer, whose self-portrait, in fact, appears on page 82 of this book. His daughter, Viola Walker, very kindly allowed me the use of his photographs.

Last of all I would like to thank Charles, my husband, who helped me with the structure and the wording of the book; without his support and encouragement this book would never have been completed.

Charlie Butler.